IOSOP
Culture

PRIMARY
CLASSROOM EDITION

For information about school-wide professional development, team training or individual coaching in the application of Loving our Students on Purpose please contact:

- www.godwinconsulting.com.au
- admin@godwinconsulting.com.au

Editor: Allison Slack
Cover Design by Ashley Beck
Interior Design and Layout by Daniel Morales
ISBN: 978-0-6459046-3-5

DEDICATION

This book is dedicated to Northside Christian College, Melbourne whose leadership and community have embraced Loving Our Students on Purpose and embedded its principles into their culture. Your commitment to connection, joy, and responsibility stands as an inspiration to others.

TABLE OF CONTENTS

BUILDING A CULTURE OF LOVE

Welcome to the LoSoP Culture Series: Classroom Edition

*Creating Classrooms Where Every Student Feels Beloved,
Chosen, and Cherished*

This series is your invitation to create something lasting in your classroom: a culture of love where every student feels beloved, chosen, and cherished. Whether you teach in a primary or secondary setting, this resource will help your class grow together in respect, responsibility, and relationships that last.

The *LoSoP Culture Series* is built on a simple but powerful truth: love changes everything. I don't mean the fluffy or feel-good kind of love, but the kind of love that shows up with boundaries, grace, and purpose––the kind of love that holds space for challenge, speaks the truth kindly, and helps students learn how to restore connection when things go wrong.

Across 40 weekly sessions, your class will explore the building blocks of a strong, connected culture. Each week focuses on a key principle of connection, drawn from four foundational pillars: *Healthy Relationships, Joyful Responsibility, Genuine Restoration,* and *Leadership Development.*

This series has been created to align with the same weekly focus used in boardrooms, staff meetings, family homes, and classrooms. That means your students will be learning the same values that are being lived out by their teachers, families, and leaders—building a shared language of love and connection across every part of their world.

What Is a Culture of Love?

A culture of love doesn't happen by accident—it's created on purpose. It's formed in the way we speak to each other, how we handle mistakes, how we set boundaries, and how we build trust through everyday moments.

This series is guided by four core truths:

1. Our goal is connection.
2. Love is a powerful choice.
3. Fear is the enemy of connection.
4. Building and protecting connection is a learning journey.

You'll return to these truths again and again as your class grows together through weekly conversations and shared practice.

The Four Pillars of a Classroom Culture of Love

Each week, you and your students will explore one or more of the four culture-building pillars:

- Healthy Relationships––where every student feels safe, valued, and included
- Joyful Responsibility––where students learn to own their actions and support their peers

- Genuine Restoration––where students practise repairing trust and reconnecting after mistakes
- Leadership Development––where students grow in confidence, courage, and positive influence

These pillars will help you create a classroom where connection is normal, not rare—and where students learn how to build community, not just follow rules.

How to Use This Series

Each session includes a core idea, simple language that's age-appropriate, space for discussion, and a weekly practice. It's designed to be flexible—you can use it in morning circles, well-being blocks, class meetings, or homeroom time. It works with whole classes or small groups, and can be adapted to suit the needs of your students.

You don't need to have all the answers—you just need to be willing to grow together.

Why It Matters

In classrooms where love leads, students thrive. They take more risks, recover from setbacks, and learn how to take care of themselves and others. They grow not just in academics, but in character, resilience, and compassion.

This series will help you create the kind of classroom where connection comes first—and everything else follows.

This is a classroom built on love—on purpose.

A NOTE FROM BERNII

Dear Educator,

Welcome to the *LoSoP Culture Series: Classroom Edition*—a resource created to support you in building a classroom where connection is the foundation, not the reward.

Teaching has always been about more than content. It's about relationships—the small, powerful moments that shape how students see themselves, each other, and the world around them. It's in your tone of voice, your body language, your ability to hold boundaries with kindness, and your commitment to repair when things go wrong.

This series is here to walk alongside you as you lead a culture of love in your classroom—one conversation at a time. Each week, you and your students will reflect on ideas that matter: how we treat people, how we take responsibility, how we repair trust, and how we grow as leaders together.

These are not just classroom management tools. They are life skills. And every time you model them, you're helping students build internal muscles for empathy, resilience, and self-awareness.

You won't need to have all the answers. You won't need to get it perfect. But your willingness to lead with love—to invite your students into real conversations, and to keep showing up with grace and courage—is enough to create something extraordinary.

Thank you for being the kind of teacher who chooses connection over control, courage over comfort, and restoration over reaction. Your students may not always have the words to say it, but the culture you create is shaping who they're becoming—and they will carry that with them long after they leave your classroom.

I'm cheering you on every step of the way.

Keep choosing connection,
Bernii

HOW TO USE THE LOSOP CULTURE SERIES: PRIMARY CLASSROOM EDITION

Creating Classrooms Where Every Student Feels Beloved, Chosen, and Cherished

The *LoSoP Culture Series: Primary Classroom Edition* is a practical, flexible resource designed to help students build meaningful relationships, take responsibility for themselves and others, and grow in personal character. Each week, you'll explore a simple idea that helps strengthen your classroom culture—one conversation at a time.

Every session helps students learn how to connect, take ownership, repair when things go wrong, and step into everyday leadership with empathy and courage.

How to Get Started

1. **Weekly Sessions**
   Each week's session includes four key sections designed to support shared learning and real-life application:

- **Learn** introduces the week's big idea using examples that are relatable and age-appropriate for students.
- **Let's Make It Real** includes a metaphor, story, or visual idea to help students connect emotionally and practically with the concept.
- **Discuss** invites students to share thoughts and reflect on how the idea shows up in their own lives and classroom relationships.
- **Do** gives students a simple, meaningful way to practise the concept together during the week.

End-of-Week Reflection

Wrap up the week with reflection questions that help students pause, notice growth, and celebrate how they've been building a stronger classroom culture.

2. **Flexible Timing**

These sessions are designed to be short, thoughtful moments you can fit into your existing routine:

- Use them as a morning check-in, a well-being circle, or an end-of-day reflection.
- Adjust the timing to suit your students' attention spans and the needs of the class. Some weeks may lead to deep conversations, while others inspire simple actions—both are powerful.

3. **Adapt for Your Students**

This resource can grow with your students:

- Use simple language and visual storytelling for younger children.
- Encourage deeper conversation and critical thinking with older or more advanced groups.

- Try partner chats, small groups, or whole-class circles depending on what works best for your setting.

4. **Create a Safe Space for Sharing**
   A culture of love starts with emotional safety.

- Let students know that all voices are welcome and there are no wrong answers when it comes to growth and connection.

- As the adult, role model vulnerability by going first—sharing your own stories or examples. This helps students feel safe to do the same.

5. **Track Growth**
   Use the End-of-Week Reflection questions as regular check-ins.

- Encourage students to think about when they used the week's idea—with their peers, teachers, or even at home.

- You might provide personal journals, drawing pages, or group charts where students can reflect and record their experiences.

6. **Integrate with Your Curriculum**
   The weekly topics work beautifully alongside your existing curriculum, especially in areas like:

- Social-emotional learning (SEL)

- Health and well-being

- Literacy, through personal writing or class read-aloud discussions

- Leadership or character education programs
   Bring the ideas into everyday learning to deepen their impact.

7. **Celebrate Progress**

   Look for moments when students practise what they've learned—even in small ways.

   - Call out kindness, courage, or responsibility when you see it.

   - Create a display or class book where students can share their reflections or weekly wins.

   - Celebrating progress reminds students that every small step matters.

8. **Revisit and Reinforce**

   Some topics will immediately click with your students, while others may take time to grow. That's okay.

   - Return to previous lessons when needed.

   - Repeat discussions or activities when challenges arise.

   - The goal isn't perfection—it's progress, together.

Final Thoughts

This series is more than a set of lessons—it's a way to build a classroom culture where every student feels seen, safe, and significant. By making space each week for reflection, conversation, and connection, you're helping your students become powerful people who know how to care for themselves and others.

Thank you for choosing to walk this journey with your class. The culture you're building today will shape your students long after they leave your room—and that is a legacy worth creating.

TOP TIP

GET READY WITH A
FEELINGS WHEEL

Before you begin the *LoSoP Culture* Series with your students, we recommend printing a large feelings wheel poster and displaying it in your classroom. You can find a variety of feelings wheels online by simply googling "Feelings Wheel"— choose one that suits the age group you're working with.

A number of topics in this series include a "How do you feel?" question. It's important to focus on the student's own experience, rather than asking, "How did that make you feel?" which can unintentionally place the responsibility for feelings outside the student. By asking "How do you feel?", we support students to take ownership of their internal emotional experiences.

Encourage students to move beyond basic labels like *sad, bad, mad,* or *glad,* and instead explore the feelings wheel to identify a more specific emotion. This simple practice helps expand their emotional vocabulary and builds their capacity to express themselves with clarity and confidence––an essential skill for connection, empathy, and self-awareness.

All emotions are good. They exist to signal that action is needed. Sometimes emotions reveal that a boundary has been crossed and invite us to take responsibility for how we protect our future boundaries. At other times they highlight a need that requires attention, or they expose a fear that has been triggered. Emotions can also be a signal that something deserves to be celebrated. Whatever the emotion, it is doing its job of communicating. Our task — and the task we teach our students — is to listen well and respond with wisdom.

PART ONE

CULTIVATING HEALTHY RELATIONSHIPS

In this section, students will learn how to build strong and meaningful connections with the people around them—classmates, teachers, friends, and family. Together, we'll explore what it means to communicate well, show empathy, build trust, and treat others with genuine respect.

Rather than just talking about relationships, students will have the chance to practise these skills in real-life ways—through stories, chats, and everyday situations. They'll begin to see that healthy relationships don't just happen—they grow when we choose to be kind, listen well, and look out for each other.

The goal? To help every student feel more confident in how they connect with others and to create a classroom culture where respect, understanding, and compassion are a natural part of daily life.

WEEK 1:

THE POWER OF LISTENING

"The quieter you become, the more you can hear."
—Winnie the Pooh

Learn:

Listening is like being a good friend in the Hundred Acre Wood—when you really listen, you demonstrate to others that they are important and valued. Sometimes we're too busy thinking about what we want to say next, but real listening means focusing on what the other person is saying. It helps us build stronger friendships because it shows we care about others' feelings and ideas.

Consider:

Imagine Tigger bouncing around and interrupting Rabbit when he's trying to talk about his garden. Rabbit feels frustrated because Tigger isn't listening, but when Tigger slows down and listens, they work together better. Good listening helps us have better friendships, just like Pooh and Tigger and their friends!

Let's Make It Real:

Talk to the person next to you about a time someone listened to you. Who was it? How did you know they were listening? How did you feel when this person listened to you?

Group Chat:

- Why is it important to listen carefully to others?
- Have you ever been in a situation where you were not listened to? What was that like for you?
- How can you practice listening to your friends this week?

Do:

This week, practice being a great listener by focusing on what others are saying without interrupting. Show you're listening by asking questions or repeating what they said.

Activity:

What Does Listening Look Like?

Draw a picture of you and your friends listening to each other. Consider:

- What does your face look like when your friend listens to you?
- What does your friend's face look like when you are listening to them?

End-of-Week Reflection:

- How did you practice listening this week?

- How did you feel when you were listened to?

- How did listening strengthen your friendships?

WEEK 2:

GIVING AND RECEIVING FEEDBACK

"To infinity and beyond!"
—Buzz Lightyear

Learn:

Just like Buzz Lightyear learns from his mistakes to become a better Space Ranger, feedback helps us improve too! Feedback isn't about criticism—it's about learning how we can get better. When we give feedback, we help others grow. When we receive feedback, we can use it to become stronger, just like Buzz when he listened to Woody's feedback!

Consider:

Imagine you're building a sandcastle with your friend at playtime, and they give you an idea on how to make it better. Instead of getting upset, you thank them and make the change, which makes your sandcastle even better. Giving and receiving feedback is all about helping each other reach new heights!

Let's Make It Real:

Talk to the person next to you about a time when feedback helped you or a friend improve something.

Group Chat:

- Why is feedback important for getting better at things?
- How can we give feedback that helps others instead of hurting their feelings?
- What's one way you can give or receive feedback kindly this week?

Do:

This week, if you receive feedback, listen and use it to grow. If you give feedback, do it in a kind and helpful way, like a friend guiding you through space!

Activity:

Playdough or Kinetic Sand Creations

- Provide each student with playdough and have them create a simple sculpture.
- After a few minutes, invite students to partner up and offer one piece of kind and constructive feedback about their partner's creation.

- Encourage students to make adjustments or additions based on the feedback they receive.
- Reflect together on how the feedback helped improve their creations.

End-of-Week Reflection:

- How did feedback help you or a friend this week?
- How did you feel when you received feedback?
- What did you learn about the importance of feedback?

WEEK 3:

THE POWER OF EMPATHY

"It's not about how fast you are, it's about how much you care."
—Lightning McQueen

Learn:

Empathy means caring about how other people feel. It's like imagining what it would be like to be in someone else's shoes—or in Lightning McQueen's case, in someone else's tires! When we use empathy, we listen, care, and help others feel better.

Yellow Trucking:

Have you ever played with a big yellow Tonka truck? It's fun to push around! But imagine if that big truck was real. It's so huge that it could squish smaller cars, like a little red Lightning McQueen car. That wouldn't feel very nice, would it?

When someone uses their big emotions like anger to get their own way or hurts others with unkind words or actions, we call it "Yellow Trucking." It's like the big truck crushing others. But when we care about how others feel, we're being like Lightning McQueen—a good friend who helps others feel special and loved.

Consider:

Imagine your friend is upset because they lost a game. Instead of saying, "Stop being sad," you could say, "I understand you're feeling upset right now." That's using empathy! It helps your friend feel heard and makes your friendship stronger.

Let's Make It Real:

Turn to the person next to you and talk about a time when someone showed empathy to you. Then, think about a time when someone acted like a Yellow Truck. Which one made you feel better?

Group Chat:

- How does empathy help us be better friends?
- Can you remember a time when empathy helped you feel better?
- What can you do when you feel like a Yellow Truck is about to come out?

Do:

This week, when something doesn't go your way, take a deep breath and try to be like Lightning McQueen. Show kindness and empathy instead of acting like a Yellow Truck.

Activity:

Yellow Truck and Lightning McQueen Role Play

- Act out two short scenes. In one scene, pretend someone is being a Yellow Truck by not listening or being unkind. Then switch and act out the same situation, but this time, pretend to be like Lightning McQueen by showing empathy and kindness.

- Talk about how each version made you feel.

End-of-Week Reflection:

- Did you show empathy to someone this week?

- Was there a time you stopped your Yellow Truck from coming out? How did it feel?

WEEK 4:

TALKING WITH KINDNESS AND SHOWING LOVE

"Some people are worth melting for."
—OLAF, *FROZEN*

Learn:

Olaf is a great friend because he knows how to show love and care. Sometimes he gives warm hugs, sometimes he spends time with his friends, and sometimes he takes time by himself to rest. Everyone feels loved in different ways—some people like hugs, others like kind words, or help with something hard, and others like when you bring them something meaningful, or when you spend time doing something together. These are called "love languages."

When we learn how our friends and family receive love, we can be better at showing we care!

Consider:

Think about Olaf in *Frozen*. He gives warm hugs and loves being with his friends. Now think about what makes *you* feel loved. Maybe it's when someone says something kind, plays with you, gives you a hug, helps you, or gives you a small gift. These are all different ways to show love and care.

Let's Make It Real:

Turn to the person next to you and talk about a time when you experienced love. Is it playing together? A high-five in the morning? A kind word?

Discuss:

- Why is it important to know how people experience love?
- How can showing love in the way someone else likes help us be better friends?

Do:

This week, try to notice how your friends and family experience love (it's okay to ask them). Then, do something kind in a way that they like—maybe playing their game, writing a card to tell them you love them, or looking for a rock to add to their collection. Just like Olaf!

Activity:

Love Language Charades

- The teacher or a student acts out one way to show love (like giving a hug, helping clean up, saying something kind, giving a pretend gift, or sitting together quietly).

- The rest of the class guesses which way they are showing care.

- Talk about which ones you like best and why.

End-of-Week Reflection:

- What did you do to show someone you care this week?

- How did you feel when you showed love to someone else?

- What's one new way you can show kindness and love next week?

WEEK 5:

SOLVING PROBLEMS TOGETHER

"I'm not a warrior. I'm just an ant. But I can help!"
— FLIK, *A BUG'S LIFE*

Learn:

Sometimes we get upset with our friends. That's called a conflict—like when two people want the same toy or don't agree on what game to play. Conflicts are normal, and we all have them. What's important is how we solve them!

When we listen, use kind words, and try to understand how the other person feels, we can work together to fix the problem and keep being friends. It's like being on the same team to solve a puzzle or a brain teaser!

Consider:

Imagine two friends arguing over whose turn it is on the swings at playtime. One says, "Let's take turns!" and the other agrees. Now both kids are smiling and playing together. That's how we solve problems as a team!

Let's Make It Real:

Turn to the person next to you and talk about a time when you had a problem with someone and you fixed it kindly. What did you do?

Discuss:

- Why is it good to fix problems peacefully?
- How do you feel when someone listens to you?
- What can you say when you and a friend both want the same thing?

Do:

This week, when a problem happens, stop and take a breath. Use your words to explain how you feel, and listen to what the other person says. Try to work it out together.

Activity:

Feelings Cards Problem Solving Game

- Create or use simple cards with pictures of faces showing emotions such as happy, sad, mad, worried, etc.

- Share a pretend problem, like two kids wanting the same swing.
- Ask: "How do you think each person feels?"
- In pairs or as a class talk about ways they could solve this problem kindly.
- Repeat with other pretend problems to practise solving problems together.

End-of-Week Reflection:

- Did you fix a problem kindly this week?
- How did you feel working together instead of getting upset?
- What is one kind word or action you can use next time there's a problem?

WEEK 6:

SHOWING RESPECT TO EVERYONE

"Ohana means family, and family means nobody gets left behind."
—LILO, *LILO & STITCH*

Learn:

Respect means treating people kindly and showing them they matter—even if they look different, think different, or like different things. In *Lilo & Stitch*, Lilo teaches us that Ohana means family, and family sticks together. That's what respect looks like!

When we show respect, we listen, take turns, use kind words, and look after each other. It helps everyone feel safe, happy, and loved.

Consider:

Imagine your friend wants to play a different game than you. Instead of saying, "That's a silly game," you say, "Okay, let's try your game first!"

That's showing respect—letting others have a turn and valuing what they like.

Let's Make It Real:

Turn to the person next to you and talk about a time when someone showed you respect. How did it make you feel? Can you think of a time when you showed respect to someone else?

Discuss:

- Why is it important to treat everyone kindly?
- What is one way you can show respect at school or at home?

Do:

This week, focus on showing respect to your classmates, teachers, and family. That might mean waiting your turn, using kind words, or listening carefully to someone's story without interrupting.

Activity:

Respect Tree Craft

- Create a big paper tree on a wall or board.
- Each student gets a paper leaf. Throughout the week, students can draw or write on a leaf the ways they have shown respect (like helping a friend, saying thank you, or sharing toys).
- Stick the leaves on the tree throughout the week to grow your "Respect Tree."

End-of-Week Reflection:

- At the end of the week, read out some of the leaves and celebrate your respectful classroom!

- How did you feel when you showed respect to others?

- What is one new way you want to practise respect next week?

WEEK 7:

BETTER TOGETHER

"Together, we can do anything."
—Barbie, *Barbie Princess Charm School*

Learn:

Teamwork means working together to get something done. It's like being on a superhero team—everyone has something special to share! When we work together, we listen to each other, share jobs, and help each other. That's what makes teamwork so powerful.

Consider:

Think about when you build a tall block tower with your friends. One person puts on the bottom blocks, another adds the middle, and some-one else puts the top on. When you work together, the tower gets fin-ished faster and taller—and everyone feels proud!

Let's Make It Real:

Talk to the person next to you about a time when you worked with someone to finish something. How did you feel? What did you like about working together?

Discuss:

- Why is working together helpful?
- How can listening make teamwork better?
- What's one way you can be a good teammate this week?

Do:

This week, focus on being a great team player. That means sharing, listening, and helping others. When someone needs help, offer a hand and do your part!

Activity:

Build It Together Challenge

- In small groups, give students a small set of blocks, cups, or craft sticks.
- The challenge: build the tallest tower or longest bridge—but they can only build by taking turns and talking about their plan first.
- After building, each group shares what helped them work well together.

End-of-Week Reflection:

- What did you do to help your team this week?

- How did you feel working together?

- What's something you want to try next time you're part of a team?

WEEK 8:

BUILDING TRUST

"Just keep swimming."
—DORY, FINDING NEMO

Learn:

Building trust means showing others they can count on you. It's like Dory in *Finding Nemo*—she keeps swimming and doesn't give up, even when things are tricky. We build trust when we are honest, keep our promises, and show up for others.

Consider:

Imagine you tell your friend, "I'll help you clean up today," and then you really do it! Your friend will experience you as safe and predictable. That's trust—doing what you say you will do.

Let's Make It Real:

Talk to the person next to you about a time when someone kept a promise to you. How did you feel? What helped you trust them more?

Discuss:

- Why is trust important in friendships?
- How does it feel when someone keeps their promise?
- What's one way you can build trust with someone this week?

Do:

This week, focus on building trust by doing what you say you will do. Be kind, show up, and keep your promises.

Activity:

Trust Jar

- Get a clear jar or container and some small objects like pom-poms, buttons, or blocks.
- Each time someone shows trust-building behaviour (like keeping a promise, helping a friend, or telling the truth), they get to add one piece to the jar.
- Watch the jar fill up during the week and celebrate how your class is growing trust together!

End-of-Week Reflection:

- What did you do this week to build trust?
- How did you feel when someone trusted you?
- What's one way you want to focus on building trust next week?

WEEK 9:

RESPONSIBLE AND CONNECTED

"With great power comes great responsibility."
—Uncle Ben, *Spider-Man*

Learn:

Being responsible means doing the things you need to do, like packing your bag or helping clean up the classroom. Having good relationships means being kind and spending time with your friends. When we do both—take care of our tasks *and* care for our friends—we feel proud and strong, just like Spider-Man!

Consider:

Imagine you really want to play outside, but your teacher asks you to tidy up first. You quickly finish your task and then go play. That's balance! You were responsible and still had fun with your friends.

Let's Make It Real:

Turn to the person next to you and talk about a time when you did your responsibilities before playing. How did you feel? What helped you do both?

Discuss:

- Why is it important to do our responsibilities before we play?
- How does being responsible help us have more fun?
- What's one thing you can do this week to balance responsibility and relationships?

Do:

This week, focus on doing your responsibilities first, then enjoy your time with friends. That way, you get things done and still have fun together!

Activity:

Balance Scale Sort

- Create a simple balance scale using a hanger and two cups or buckets.
- Give students picture cards of tasks (like brushing teeth, packing up, helping a friend, playing a game).
- Let them take turns choosing one "responsibility" and one "relationship" card to place on each side.
- Talk about how to keep the balance and why both are important.

End-of-Week Reflection:

- What did you do to balance work and fun this week?

- How did you feel when you got your responsibilities done and still had time with friends?

- What's something you want to focus on balancing next week?

WEEK 10:

SUPPORTIVE FRIENDSHIPS USING THE EMPOWERMENT MODEL

"You've got a friend in me."
—Woody, *Toy Story*

Learn:

Being a good friend doesn't mean doing everything for your friends—it means helping them figure out what to do on their own. Think about Woody and Buzz from *Toy Story*: they ask each other questions, share ideas, and encourage each other when things are tough. The Empowerment Model helps us do the same!

The 6 Steps of the Empowerment Model:

1. **Empathy**: Show that you care about how your friend feels. You could say, "I'm sorry that happened," or, "That sounds like it was scary."

2. **Empower**: Ask your friend, "What are you going to do?" This helps them start thinking of ways to solve the problem and sends the message that you believe they can.

3. **Explore**: Ask them, "Have you tried anything already?" This gets them to think about what they've done so far and what worked or didn't work.

4. **Educate**: Offer some ideas or advice, but only if they want it. You might say, "I have some ideas if you'd like to hear them." This lets them know you're there to help, but they're in charge of deciding.

5. **Expect**: Ask, "What are you going to do now?" This helps your friend make a plan for what they're going to do next.

6. **Encourage**: Cheer them on! Say, "Let me know how you get on." This reminds them that you're supporting them all the way.

Let's Make It Real Activity:

Role play with the person next to you. One person thinks of a problem and the other person uses the Empowerment Model to help guide the conversation.

Discuss:

*   Why is it important to let friends figure things out on their own?
*   How can asking questions help your friends feel stronger?
*   What's one way you can support a friend using the Empowerment Model this week?

Do:

This week, if a friend has a problem, ask them questions and encourage them to find their own solution instead of fixing it for them.

End-of-Week Reflection:

- How did supporting a friend using the Empowerment Model help them this week?
- What did you learn about being a supportive friend?

PART TWO

BUILDING JOYFUL RESPONSIBILITY

In this section, students will discover that taking responsibility for their actions doesn't have to feel like a heavy burden—in fact, it can be something that brings confidence, growth, and even joy!

Through simple, real-life lessons and meaningful conversations, students will learn that responsibility isn't just about following rules—it's about making thoughtful choices, owning their part, and understanding how their actions affect others.

We want students to see responsibility as something *they* get to carry with pride—not something that's forced on them. When we choose to be responsible, we build trust, grow stronger relationships, and learn more about who we are and who we want to become.

WEEK 11:

OWNING YOUR ACTIONS

"Everything is cool when you're part of a team."
—*The LEGO Movie*

Learn:

Owning your actions means saying, "I did that," whether it was something kind or a mistake. When we take responsibility, we show we're growing up, just like Emmet in *The LEGO Movie*! He learns to be brave, fix his mistakes, and work with others. We all make mistakes sometimes—but when we own up, we can make things right.

Consider:

Imagine you're playing with LEGO and knock over your friend's tower by accident. Instead of saying, "You put it too close to mine," you say, "Oops, I knocked it over. I'll help fix it." That's owning your actions! It shows your friend you care and want to make things better.

Let's Make It Real:

Turn to the person next to you and talk about a time you made a mistake and took responsibility. How did it feel when you were honest and fixed it?

Discuss:

- Why is it good to say sorry when we've done something wrong?
- How does it feel when someone else takes responsibility?
- What's one way you can own your actions this week?

Do:

This week, focus on owning your actions. If you make a mess, say so. If you forget something, be honest. That's how we grow and show we care!

Activity:

Build and Rebuild Game

- In pairs or small groups, students build a simple LEGO or block tower.
- One person gently knocks it over (on purpose or by accident) and practises saying, "I'm sorry, I knocked it over. Can I help rebuild it?"
- Switch roles and practise again.
- After, talk about how it felt to own the action and make it right.

End-of-Week Reflection:

- What did you do this week to own your actions?

- How did you feel when you told the truth and made it better?

- What's something you want to focus on next time a mistake happens?

WEEK 12:

POWERFUL PEOPLE, POWERFUL RELATIONSHIPS

"In every job that must be done, there is an element of fun."
—MARY POPPINS

Learn:

In friendships, we can act in powerful or powerless ways. Being powerful means using kind words, making good choices, and working together. Being powerless means trying to control others or letting others do everything for us. Mary Poppins is powerful because she takes care of what she needs to do, but she also makes it fun and includes everyone.

There are three ways people might act with each other:

1. **Powerless + Powerless** — Both people try to be the boss and argue.

2. **Powerless + Powerful** — One person makes all the choices while the other does nothing.
3. **Powerful + Powerful** — Both people listen, share, and work together like a team.

When we are powerful in our relationships, we are kind, take turns, and help each other.

Consider:

Imagine you and a friend are pretending to clean up like Mary Poppins. If you both start telling each other what to do and don't listen, you might get upset and the job won't be much fun. That's being powerless. But if you both take turns, sing a little song, and work together, it becomes fun and gets done quicker. That's being powerful!

Let's Make It Real:

Turn to the person next to you and talk about a time when you were powerful in a game by sharing or helping. How did it feel?

Discuss:

- What does it feel like when you and a friend both act powerful and kind?
- Have you ever been in a game where someone acted powerless and tried to boss everyone around?
- How can we be like Mary Poppins and work together in powerful ways?

Do:

This week, focus on being powerful in your relationships. That means making kind choices, using your voice, and working with others instead of trying to be the boss.

Activity:

Tidy-Up Teamwork Game

- Set up a small play area with pretend mess (e.g. soft toys, blocks, scarves).

- In pairs or small groups, students are told they have 2 minutes to "clean up like Mary Poppins."

- They must take turns, share the jobs, and encourage each other––no bossing allowed!

- Play cheerful music to make it fun, just like in the movie!

- After, reflect on how it felt to work powerfully together instead of trying to take control or waiting for others to do it all.

End-of-Week Reflection:

- What did you do to work kindly and powerfully with someone this week?

- How did it feel when you shared ideas and took turns?

- What's one way you want to be powerful next time you play with a friend?

WEEK 13:

CHOOSING LOVE OVER FEAR

"You don't have to be the bad guy."
—EMMET, *THE LEGO MOVIE*

Learn:

Sometimes when we feel scared, sad, or unsure, we might act in ways that push people away. That's fear talking. But when we choose love, we try to stay kind, gentle, and connected—even when things feel tricky.

Fear says, "Go away." Love says, "I'm here for you."

When we choose love, we help people feel safe and cared for—just like when Emmet helps his friends work together and feel brave.

Consider:

Imagine a friend makes a mistake during a game and feels upset. If you laugh or ignore them, they feel more alone. That's fear. But if you say, "It's okay, we all make mistakes—let's try again together," you help them feel better. That's love.

Let's Make It Real:

Talk to the person next to you about a time when someone was kind to you when you were upset. How did it feel when they chose love instead of fear?

Discuss:

- How does fear sometimes make us hide our feelings or push people away?
- How does it feel when someone chooses love and helps you feel safe?
- What's one way you can choose love this week?

Do:

This week, focus on choosing love, even when things feel a little scary or hard. That might mean being kind to someone who made a mistake, or staying close to a friend who feels sad.

Activity:

Love vs. Fear Sorting Game

- Prepare a mix of simple scenarios (on cards or read aloud), like:
  - A friend drops their lunch.
  - You make a mistake in front of the class.
  - Someone is sitting alone.

- As a class, decide: Is this a moment to choose fear (hide, walk away) or love (help, stay close)?
- Discuss the loving choice for each one.

End-of-Week Reflection:

- What did you do this week to choose love?
- How did it feel when you helped someone or stayed kind?
- What's one way you can keep choosing love over fear next week?

WEEK 14:

FREEDOM THROUGH BOUNDARIES

"You are a toy! You can't fly!"
—Buzz Lightyear, *Toy Story*

Learn:

Boundaries are like invisible fences that help keep us safe. They are the rules that show us where it's safe to go, how to treat others, and how to have fun without getting hurt. In *Toy Story*, Buzz Lightyear thinks he can fly, but Woody reminds him, "You are a toy! You can't fly!" Buzz learns that knowing his limits helps him be the best toy he can be. Just like Buzz, when we know our limits and follow rules, we can stay safe and enjoy more freedom.

When we follow rules and respect boundaries, we can run, play, and explore with more freedom—because we know we're safe.

Consider:

Imagine you're at the playground. There's a fence around the play area. You can run fast, climb high, and play games—and you don't have to worry, because the fence keeps you safe. But if you climb over the fence, you might get lost or hurt. That's why boundaries help us enjoy our freedom!

Let's Make It Real:

Talk to the person next to you about a time when a rule helped keep you safe or made playing more fun. How did it feel to have that safety?

Discuss:

- Why do we have rules at school or home?
- How do rules help us have more fun?
- What could happen if we don't follow the rules?

Do:

This week, focus on respecting boundaries like staying where it's safe, following classroom routines, or using kind hands and words. Notice how these rules help everyone enjoy their day.

Activity:

Option 1: Safe Zone Adventure

- Set up an indoor or outdoor obstacle course with cones or markers. Create a clear "boundary" (rope, chalk line, or tape) that students must stay inside.

- Give them different tasks (hop like a bunny, tiptoe like a mouse, crawl like a cat) — but they must stay in the safe zone!
- Talk after about how the boundary helped everyone stay safe and enjoy the game.

Option 2: Boundary Hunt Walk

- Take students on a walk around the school to find different boundaries (like fences, staffroom doors, gates, or the edge of the car park).
- At each spot, ask: "Can we go past here? Why or why not?"
- Discuss how each boundary helps keep them safe and lets them play and learn without getting hurt.

End-of-Week Reflection:

- What did you do this week to respect boundaries?
- How did it feel to play and learn inside safe rules?
- What's one boundary you want to remember next week to keep having fun?

WEEK 15:

RESPECT & CONNECT

"I know what to do--be kind!"

—Bluey

Learn:

Respect means being kind and showing others that they matter. Imagine your relationship with a friend is like a rope. You hold one end, and they hold the other. If you both hold on gently and kindly, the rope stays strong. But if someone lets go or pulls too hard, the rope can break or feel like it's made of tissue—soft and easy to tear.

You're only responsible for your own end of the rope. That means even if someone else is unkind, you can still choose to be respectful and keep your end strong.

Consider:

Think about playing a game where you and a friend have to hold a ribbon and walk together. If you both hold it gently and move together, it works! But if someone lets go or pulls too hard, it doesn't work anymore. That's like respect—it only works when we both try, but you can still do your part!

Let's Make It Real:

Talk to the person next to you about a time when you were respectful, even if someone else was not. How did it feel to hold your end of the rope?

Discuss:

- What does it mean to hold your end of the rope?
- How does it feel when someone is respectful to you?
- What can you do this week to keep your relationships strong like a rope, not weak like tissue?

Do:

This week, focus on being respectful—even if things don't go your way. Use kind words, take turns, and be a good listener.

Activity:

Tissue and Rope Walk Game

- Set up an obstacle course inside or outside the classroom.

- In pairs, give one group a tissue to hold between them and walk across the room (it will likely tear!).
- Then give them a piece of string or ribbon and ask them to do it again.
- Talk about which one felt stronger and why. Explain how being respectful helps make our friendships strong like a rope.

End-of-Week Reflection:

- What did you do to be respectful this week?
- How did it feel to keep your end of the rope strong?
- What will you do next week to keep your relationships strong?

WEEK 16:

GROWING AND TAKING RESPONSIBILITY

"Even miracles take a little time."
—Fairy Godmother, *Cinderella*

Learn:

Taking responsibility means doing your best to grow and learn, even when things are tricky. It's like learning to ride a bike or zip up your jacket—it takes time and effort, but you can do it!

Remember the Empowerment Model? Did you know you can also use it to help yourself grow? Here's how:

1. **Empathy**: Notice how you feel and say, "It's okay, I'm still learning."

2. **Empower**: Ask, "What do I want to achieve?"

3. **Explore**: Think about what you've already tried. What helped? What didn't? Is there anything getting in your way or making it tricky?

4. **Educate**: Learn something new that can help you grow. Who can you ask? Where can you look? Learning helps you take the next step!

5. **Expect**: Make a plan to try a new idea.

6. **Encourage**: Cheer yourself on and check how you're doing!

Consider:

Imagine you want to get better at tying your shoes. At first, it's hard! But you keep trying, ask for help, and practise every day. That's taking responsibility and using the Empowerment Model to grow!

Let's Make It Real:

Talk to the person next to you about something you're learning to do. How could these steps help you keep going?

Discuss:

- How does it feel to learn something new, even when it's hard?
- Who can help you when you want to grow?
- What step will you focus on this week?

Do:

This week, focus on growing in one area—like listening better, packing your bag, or learning something new. Use the Empowerment steps to help you!

Activity:

My Growth Steps Poster

- Give each student a simple poster template with six boxes (one for each step).

- Ask them to choose something they want to get better at (e.g., drawing, being kind, zipping their jacket).

- They draw or write what they will do for each step.

- Display the posters in the classroom to remind everyone that we're all growing!

End-of-Week Reflection:

- What did you choose to grow in this week?

- How did it feel to take responsibility and keep going?

- What's one step you want to keep using next week?

WEEK 17:

LEARNING FROM MISTAKES WITH LOVE

"Anyone can cook!"
—Remy, *Ratatouille*

Learn:

Everyone makes mistakes––even great chefs like Remy the rat! In *Ratatouille*, Remy burns food, spills soup, and sometimes messes things up. But instead of giving up, he learns, tries again, and gets better each time.

When we make a mistake, we have a choice. We can hide it (that's fear), or we can be honest, fix it, and learn from it (that's love). Love means giving ourselves and others the chance to grow.

Consider:

Imagine you're helping in the kitchen and you spill flour everywhere. You can choose to be scared and hide, or you can say, "Oops! I made a mess," and help clean it up. When we respond with love and honesty, we get better and braver.

Let's Make It Real:

Talk to the person next to you about a time you made a mistake. Did someone help you fix it with love? How did that feel?

Discuss:

- Why is it okay to make mistakes?
- How does it feel when someone helps you kindly instead of getting upset?
- How can we help others when they make mistakes?

Do:

This week, if you make a mistake, stop and take a breath. Tell the truth, try to fix it, and be kind to yourself. That's how we grow with love!

Activity:

Make-Your-Own Trail Mix (Mistake-Friendly Cooking!)

- Give each child a small bowl and several snack options (like cereal, dried fruit, pretzels, popcorn, mini marshmallows).
- Let them scoop and mix their own trail mix.

- If they spill or choose a mix they don't love, they get to talk about what they'd change next time—it's all part of learning!
- Celebrate that mistakes help us get better—even in the kitchen!

End-of-Week Reflection:

- What mistake did I learn from this week?
- How did it feel to be kind to myself instead of hiding it?
- What will I do next time to grow with love and courage?

WEEK 18:

HELPING EACH OTHER GROW

"You are my greatest adventure."
—Mr. Incredible, *The Incredibles*

Learn:

Sometimes we need a little help to reach our goals, and that's okay! Having a buddy—or an accountability partner—is like having your very own superhero sidekick. They cheer you on, remind you of what you want to do, and help you keep going, even when it gets tricky.

When we help each other, we both grow stronger!

Consider:

Imagine you and a friend both want to practise learning a new skill like kicking a ball or riding a bike. You remind each other to practice every morning, and you say, "You can do it!" That makes it more fun and helps you get better faster.

Let's Make It Real:

Talk to the person next to you about something you're learning right now. How have your parents, siblings, or friends cheered you on or helped you keep going?

Discuss:

- How can a partner help you stick with your goal?
- What does it feel like when someone cheers you on?
- What makes a good helping partner?

Do:

This week, pick a buddy and choose one small thing you both want to get better at. Some ideas could be making your own sandwich, keeping your desk or bag tidy, holding your pencil correctly, or using kind words. Check in with each other every day and give high-fives when you make an effort!

Activity:

Super Buddy Chart

- Give each buddy pair a simple chart with five boxes (one for each day).
- Each time they check in and help each other work on their goal, they colour a box or add a sticker.
- At the end of the week, celebrate working together and growing as a team!

Buddy Celebration Card

- At the end of the week, invite each student to make a card for their buddy.
- Inside the card, they can draw a picture and write a simple note like, "You did a great job!" or "Thank you for helping me!"
- Students give their cards to each other during a short class celebration.

End-of-Week Reflection:

- What did you and your buddy work on this week?
- How did it feel to help each other?
- What's something else you'd like to work on with a partner next time?

WEEK 19:

STICKING WITH IT

"Adventure is out there!"
—Ellie, *Up*

Learn:

Self-discipline means doing what you know is right, even when it's hard. In *Up*, Ellie and Carl dream of a big adventure, and Carl keeps working toward that dream even when it takes a long time. That's self-discipline—not giving up and doing the right thing even when other things try to distract you.

When we show self-discipline, we make choices that help us grow—like putting our things away, practising something new, or finishing our work before we play.

Consider:

Imagine you're learning to write in cursive. At first, the letters feel wobbly and tricky. You might want to stop, but instead you keep trying every day. Soon, your letters get smoother and clearer. That's self-discipline—practising something hard even when it takes time.

Let's Make It Real:

Talk to the person next to you about something that was hard to learn but you kept going. How did it feel when you reached your goal?

Discuss:

- Why is it important to keep trying when things are tricky?
- What helps you stay focused when you want to stop?
- How can we practise self-discipline at school or home?

Do:

This week, practise self-discipline by choosing one small goal—like doing your chores before using technology, asking your mum or dad about their day, or being at the car ready for school before your parent(s)—and keep going, even when it's hard.

Activity:

Bubble Name Writing Challenge

- Give each student a bubble-letter version of their own name to trace and decorate.

- Then, they practise writing their name neatly underneath using their best handwriting.
- Celebrate their effort and talk about how it felt to stick with something that takes practice!

End-of-Week Reflection:

- What goal did you work on this week?
- How did it feel to stick with it?
- What's something else you want to practise next?

WEEK 20:

JOYFUL RESPONSIBILITY

"The things that make me different are the things that make me ME."
—PIGLET, *WINNIE THE POOH*

Learn:

Joyful responsibility means taking care of your jobs with a happy heart. It's like helping clean up the playroom or feeding your pet before play-time. In the Hundred Acre Wood, Piglet and his friends always try their best to help, even when the jobs are small. When we do what needs to be done first, playtime feels even better!

Consider:

Imagine you want to play outside, but first you need to tidy your toys. You decide to do it quickly and happily. Then, when you play, it feels extra fun because you finished your job first. That's joyful responsibility!

Let's Make It Real:

Talk to the person next to you about a time when you did a job before playing. How did it feel to be responsible and then have fun?

Discuss:

- Why is it important to do our jobs before play?
- How can being responsible help us enjoy playtime more?
- What jobs can you do that make you feel proud?

Do:

This week, practise joyful responsibility by choosing one job to do each day before you play—like packing your bag, putting your shoes away, or setting the table.

Activity:

Washing Machine Adventure!

- Ask a grown-up at home (like Mum or Dad) to show you how to use the washing machine.
- Talk about what the buttons do and help press them.
- You can even help sort the clothes or match the socks!
- It's a fun way to learn responsibility and help your family.

End-of-Week Reflection:

- What job did you do before playing this week?
- How did it feel to finish your job first?
- What's another way you can practise joyful responsibility at home or school?

PART THREE

ACHIEVING GENUINE RESTORATION

This section is all about learning how to repair relationships when things go wrong—because let's face it, we all make mistakes sometimes.

Students will explore how to take responsibility when they've hurt someone, how to listen and make things right, and how to rebuild trust over time. Instead of focusing on blame or punishment, we'll focus on courage, honesty, and healing.

Restoration isn't about being perfect—it's about being real. When students learn how to own their part and care about how others feel, relationships grow stronger than ever. Together, we'll build a culture where making things right is seen as an act of strength, not weakness.

WEEK 21:

THE ART OF APOLOGY

"I am sorry for what I did. I learned my lesson and I won't do it again."
—Bing Bong, *Inside Out*

Learn:

Saying sorry is more than just words—it's about meaning it in your heart. When we hurt someone, even by accident, we can help fix the problem by saying sorry, taking responsibility, and asking how to make it better.

A real apology shows we care about our friends and want to keep our relationships strong.

A good apology sounds like this:

- "I am sorry for _____ (say what you did)."

- "If that happened to me, I would feel _____ (say how you think they felt)."
- "Next time I will _____ (say what you will do differently)."
- "I want you to feel _____ (say how you hope they will feel after your apology)."

Consider:

Imagine you were running and bumped into a friend, and they fell down. You stop, help them up, and say:

"I am sorry for bumping into you. If that happened to me, I would feel hurt and surprised. Next time I will walk more carefully. I want you to feel safe and cared for."

That's a caring apology—it helps your friend feel better and helps you stay connected.

Let's Make It Real:

Talk to the person next to you about a time when you said sorry. How did apologising protect your connection?

Discuss:

- Why is it important to say sorry when we make a mistake?
- How do you feel when someone says sorry to you?
- What can we do to show our apology is real?

Do:

This week, if something goes wrong, practise giving a kind and honest apology. Think about how to help make things right, not just say the words.

Activity:

Apology Role Play

- In pairs, take turns pretending to make a mistake (like stepping on someone's foot or knocking over blocks).

- Practise saying a real apology using these steps:

    - "I am sorry for _____."
    - "If that happened to me, I would feel _____."
    - "Next time I will _____."
    - "I want you to feel _____."

- Use a printed feelings wheel to help you choose the right words. Your teacher can print one out for you!

- After each turn, switch roles. Talk about how it felt to give and receive a caring apology.

End-of-Week Reflection:

- Did you need to say sorry this week? How did it help?

- How did it feel when someone said sorry to you?

- What will you do next time you need to make things right?

WEEK 22:

FORGIVENESS AND MOVING FORWARD

"I never look back, darling. It distracts from the now."
—EDNA MODE, *THE INCREDIBLES*

Learn:

Forgiveness means letting go of hurt and choosing to be kind again. It's a bit like blowing bubbles—when we forgive, we let our upset feelings float away, just like bubbles drifting up into the sky. We don't hold onto them anymore. Everyone makes mistakes, and sometimes people hurt our feelings. When we forgive, we decide not to stay upset—we move forward and give friendship another chance.

Forgiving doesn't mean we forget what happened, but it means we don't stay angry.

Consider:

Imagine you're playing soccer and your friend accidentally trips you over while trying to get the ball. You fall and feel a bit sore and upset. Your friend runs over and says:

"I'm really sorry for tripping you while we were playing. If that happened to me, I'd feel hurt and maybe a little angry. Next time, I'll watch where I'm running and slow down near other players. I hope you feel safe playing with me again."

You could stay mad, or you could choose to forgive them. You say, "I forgive you," and the two of you keep playing and having fun. Forgiveness helps you feel better and brings your friendship back together.

Let's Make It Real:

Talk to the person next to you about a time when you forgave someone or when someone forgave you. How did it make you feel?

Discuss:
- Why is it important to forgive others?
- How does it feel when someone forgives you?
- What happens if we stay angry for a long time?

Do:

This week, if someone upsets you, try choosing forgiveness. You can say, "I forgive you," or show it by being kind and letting go of the hurt.

Activity:

Let It Go Bubbles

- Go outside and blow bubbles.
- As each bubble floats away, imagine letting go of something that upset you.
- Say, "I let it go," as each bubble drifts off.
- Talk together about how it feels to forgive and move forward.

End-of-Week Reflection:

- Did you forgive someone this week? How did it make you feel?
- How did forgiveness help your friendship?
- What will you do next time someone makes a mistake?

WEEK 23:

RESTORING TRUST

"True friends are never apart, maybe in distance but never in heart."
—THE FOX AND THE HOUND

Learn:

Sometimes friends make mistakes and it hurts our feelings. When that happens, trust can feel broken or shaky, like something that needs to be gently repaired. Restoring trust means trying to make things right again. We do this by being honest, showing kindness, and doing what we say we will do.

It takes time, but with care and effort, trust can grow strong again.

Consider:

Imagine you told your friend a secret, but they shared it with someone else. When this happened, you might have felt disappointed or unsure if you could trust them again. You may decide not to share another secret with them until they show you they can be trusted. You'll know they're trustworthy when they stop telling you other people's secrets too.

Let's Make It Real:

Talk to the person next to you about a time when you had to fix trust with someone. What did you do that helped?

Discuss:

- Why is trust important in friendships?
- How can we show someone they can trust us again?
- What helps trust grow strong after it's been hurt?

Do:

This week, if you have a problem with a friend, practise rebuilding trust by being honest, kind, and keeping your promises.

Activity:

Trust Heart Puzzle

- Give each student a paper heart cut into 4 puzzle pieces.
- They write or draw one thing on each piece that helps rebuild trust (like saying sorry, telling the truth, being kind, or trying again).
- They put the pieces together and decorate their heart.
- Talk as a class about how each piece helps fix and grow trust.

End-of-Week Reflection:

- Did I work on rebuilding trust this week?

- What did I do to help someone trust me again?

- How did it feel to fix a friendship?

WEEK 24:

SECOND CHANCES

"The only mistake is the one from which we learn nothing."
— CHIEF BOGO, ZOOTOPIA

Learn:

A second chance means getting to try again after something didn't go well. Everyone makes mistakes, but what matters is that we learn from them and try to do better next time. Second chances help us show that we've grown and want to make things right.

When we give others a second chance, we're helping them grow too.

Consider:

Imagine you promised to feed the class pet but forgot. Your teacher talks with you and gives you another turn the next week. You make a plan to remember and take extra care. This second chance helps you show that you're responsible and willing to learn.

Let's Make It Real:

Talk to the person next to you about a time when you got a second chance or gave someone else one. What did you learn?

Discuss:

- Why are second chances important?
- How can second chances help us grow?
- What should we do when someone gives us a second chance?

Do:

This week, if someone makes a mistake, think about giving them a second chance. Encourage them to try again and do better.

Activity:

Second Chance Steps

- On a small sheet of paper, draw 4 big stepping stones.
- Label the stones: 1) What did I want to do? 2) What went wrong? 3) What will I do differently? 4) What result am I aiming for?
- Students draw or write their answers on each step.
- Use the stepping stones to talk about how we grow after mistakes and what we're working toward with a second chance.

End-of-Week Reflection:

- Did I give or receive a second chance this week?

- What did I do to make the most of that chance?

- How did it feel to try again or help someone else do better?

WEEK 25:

TAKING RESPONSIBILITY IN FRIENDSHIPS

"A true hero isn't measured by the size of his strength,
but by the strength of his heart."
—Zeus, Hercules

Learn:

Being a good friend means taking responsibility for your actions. If you do something that upsets someone, you can choose to be honest and fix it. Taking responsibility means saying sorry, making it right, and showing your friend that they matter to you.

Good friends own up to their mistakes because they care about keeping the friendship strong.

Consider:

Imagine you got upset and said something unkind to your friend at lunch. You feel regretful afterwards, so you decide to talk to them and clean up the heart mess. That's taking responsibility and showing you care.

Let's Make It Real:

Talk to the person next to you about a time when you had to take responsibility in a friendship. What did you do that helped?

Discuss:

- Why is it important to take responsibility when we make a mistake?
- How can saying sorry help a friendship heal?
- What else can we do to be a responsible friend?

Do:

This week, practise being a responsible friend. If something goes wrong, take ownership, apologise, and try to fix it with kind actions.

Activity:

Friendship Responsibility Comic Strip

- Give each student a paper with 4 blank boxes, like a comic strip.
- In Box 1, draw or write what happened that caused a problem in a friendship.

- In Box 2, show how the friend may have felt.
- In Box 3, show someone taking responsibility (like saying sorry or making it right).
- In Box 4, draw the friends playing or talking again after restoring connection.
- Invite students to share their comics with a partner and talk about what they learned.

End-of-Week Reflection:

- Did I take responsibility in a friendship this week?
- How did my actions help fix the problem?
- What did I learn about being a good friend?

WEEK 26:

POWERFUL FRIENDSHIPS

"The most important thing is that we stick together."
—Lilo, *Lilo & Stitch*

Learn:

Even good friends have arguments sometimes. But instead of trying to be right or win, we can listen carefully and care about the other person's heart. Repairing relationships isn't about proving a point—it's about understanding, listening, and choosing connection. When we listen well and stop trying to be right all the time, we make space for friendship to grow.

Consider:

Draw a big number 6 on a piece of paper and lay it on the floor between two students facing each other. What do you see? One says it's a 6. The other says it's a 9. Have the students explain their point, because from where they are standing, both of them are right! Then, invite them to walk around and stand where the other person was standing. Now they can see the number from the other person's point of view too!

Now, slide the paper so it's in front of them and they're standing shoulder to shoulder, looking at it from the same side. Suddenly, the shape doesn't look like a 6 or a 9—it looks like a snail! (Add two little antennae to the top and the round part of the number is the shell.)

Sometimes, arguments happen because we're looking at things from different angles. When we stop arguing, stand beside each other, and really listen, we can turn the problem into something we work on *together*—like spotting a snail in the classroom. Instead of blaming each other, we work together to gently take it back to the garden where it belongs.

Let's Make It Real:

Talk to the person next to you about a time when you had to fix a friendship. What helped make things better?

Discuss:
- Why is it important to listen when someone is upset?
- What happens when we focus on being right instead of caring?
- How does listening help fix a friendship?

Do:

This week, think about any friendships that need repair. Use the 6 and 9 activity to help you stop and think: What is my perspective? What might their perspective be? Then, try talking to the person and work together to fix things kindly and honestly.

Activity:

6 and 9 Snail Drawing

- Ask students to think of a time they had a disagreement or problem with someone — it could be with a friend, a teacher, or even a parent.

- Give them a piece of paper and have them draw a big 6 on one side and a big 9 on the other.

- On the 6 side, they write or draw what they were thinking and feeling.

- On the 9 side, they write or draw what the other person might have been thinking and feeling.

- Once both sides are done, they slide the paper so both the 6 and 9 are sideways, and turn it into a snail with a head and antennae.

- Talk about how understanding both sides of a problem can help us carry it gently, like a snail, and work together to make things right.

End-of-Week Reflection:

- Did I repair a friendship this week?

- What step helped the most?

- How did it feel to reconnect with someone after a problem?

WEEK 27:

BECOMING A POWERFUL PERSON

"You don't have to go into battle to be a hero. Every time
you do what's right, you are a hero."
—Mulan

Learn:

Being a powerful person doesn't mean being the boss of others. It means being in charge of yourself. Powerful people make good choices, even when things are hard. They stay calm, use kind words, and take responsibility for what they do and say.

When you control your actions and emotions, you show strength from the inside.

Consider:

Imagine someone pushed in front of you in line. You feel upset. A powerless reaction would be to yell or push back. But a powerful person stays calm and says, "I was here first. Can you please wait your turn?" That shows you're in control of yourself, even when others are not.

Let's Make It Real:

Talk to the person next to you about a time when you stayed calm or made a good choice, even when something was hard.

Discuss:

- What does it mean to be powerful on the inside?
- How can staying calm help in tricky situations?
- What are some things you can say or do to show you are powerful?

Do:

This week, focus on being a powerful person. Practise using calm words, taking deep breaths when you're upset, and making choices that show you're in control.

Activity:

My Circle of Control

- Give each student a sheet of paper with two circles drawn—one small circle inside a bigger one.
- In the small circle ("What I Can Control"), they write or draw things like: my words, my actions, my attitude, my effort.
- In the bigger circle ("What I Can't Control"), they draw or write things like: what others say, the weather, someone else's choices.

- Talk about how powerful people focus on what's inside their circle—the things they *can* control.
- Students can decorate their circles with colour and pictures to help them remember.

End-of-Week Reflection:

- Did I make powerful choices this week?
- What helped me stay calm or kind?
- How did it feel to be in control of myself, even when things were tricky?

WEEK 28:

RESTORING SELF-RESPECT

"You're stronger than you think."
—Hiccup, *How to Train Your Dragon*

Learn:

Self-respect means treating yourself kindly and remembering that you matter, even when you make mistakes. Everyone gets things wrong sometimes. What's important is that we learn from it and keep going. Restoring self-respect means picking yourself back up, trying again, and being proud of your effort.

Consider:

Imagine you forgot to bring your homework. You feel upset and embarrassed. But instead of saying, "I'm bad at school," you say, "I will bring it tomorrow." You write yourself a note to remember next time. That's how you show self-respect—you forgive yourself and choose to do better.

Let's Make It Real:

Talk to the person next to you about a time you made a mistake but kept going. What helped you feel better about yourself?

Discuss:

- Why is self-respect important?
- What does it feel like when you're not kind to yourself?
- How can you treat yourself with respect, even when things are hard?

Do:

This week, practise being kind to yourself. If you make a mistake, stop and say something kind like, "It's okay, I'm still learning."

Activity:

Self-Respect Shield

- Give each student a shield outline with four sections.
- In each section, they draw or write:
    1. A mistake I've made.
    2. What I learned from it.
    3. A kind thing I can say to myself.
    4. What I'll do next time.
- Decorate the shield with colours and symbols that make them feel strong and brave.

End-of-Week Reflection:

- Did I treat myself with kindness this week?

- How did it feel to show myself respect?

- What did I learn about bouncing back from mistakes?

WEEK 29:

TAKING INITIATIVE WITH THE EMPOWERMENT MODEL

*"If you only do what you can do, you will
never be more than you are now."*
—Master Shifu, *Kung Fu Panda*

Learn:

Taking initiative means choosing to act when something needs to be done. It means saying, "I can do something about this," instead of waiting for someone else or blaming the group for not doing the work. When we use the Empowerment Model, we take control of our own actions and help others do the same.

Teacher Note: Don't forget to display the Empowerment Model poster in your room for students to see during the week!

Quick Refresh: The 6 Steps of the Empowerment Model:

1. **Empathy**: I care about what's happening. ("Oh no, how do you feel?" — You might want to use the feelings wheel to help name your emotion.)

2. **Empower**: I ask, "What are you going to do?"

3. **Explore**: I ask, "What have you tried so far?"

4. **Educate**: I offer ideas and listen. ("Would you like a suggestion?")

5. **Expect**: I ask, "What are you going to do now?"

6. **Encourage**: I cheer you on. ("We've got this!")

Consider:

Imagine your group project is falling behind. Instead of waiting, you take initiative:

- You start with **Empathy** and ask, "Does anyone else feel stuck, frustrated, or worried?

- **Empower**: You ask, "What are we going to do about it?"

- **Explore**: You ask, "What have we already tried?"

- **Educate**: You offer ideas and say, "Would you like a suggestion?" or "I'd like to hear your suggestions"

- **Expect**: You ask, "what shall we do next?"

- **Encourage**: You say, "Let's do this together! We've got this!"

This is what powerful people do—they see a problem, care about it, and empower action.

Let's Make It Real:

Talk to the person next to you about a time when you saw a problem and took action. What did you do? How did it help?

Discuss:

- What does it mean to take initiative?
- How does the Empowerment Model help you solve problems?
- What is one step you can use this week?

Do:

This week, if you see a problem in your group, class, or playground—don't wait. Use the Empowerment Model and take action!

Activity:

Empowerment Scenario Skits

- Divide students into small groups.
- Give each group a common classroom or playground problem (e.g. someone feeling left out, a messy area, arguing over supplies).
- Each group uses the 6 steps of the Empowerment Model to create a short skit that shows how they could respond to the problem.
- Groups perform their skits for the class, and the audience identifies which Empowerment Model steps they noticed being used.

End-of-Week Reflection:

- Did I take initiative this week?
- What step of the Empowerment Model helped the most?
- How did it feel to be the one who made a difference?

WEEK 30:

BEING A ROLE MODEL

"Remember who you are."
—Mufasa, *The Lion King*

Learn:

A role model is someone others look up to. They show what it means to be kind, brave, honest, and responsible. Being a role model doesn't mean being perfect—it means making good choices, even when no one is watching. When you act in a way that helps others learn and grow, you're being a leader.

Consider:

Imagine someone is always kind to others, follows the rules, and helps clean up without being asked. Other kids start doing the same because they see that good behaviour. That person has become a role model—by doing what's right, they inspire others.

Let's Make It Real:

Talk to the person next to you about someone who sets a great example. What do they do that makes them a role model?

Discuss:

- Why is it important to set a good example?
- Can you think of a time when someone's actions made you want to do better?
- How can you be a role model in your classroom or playground?

Do:

This week, think about what kind of role model you want to be. Make choices that show kindness, responsibility, and courage—even when it's hard.

Activity:

Role Model Footsteps

- Have each student trace their own foot on a piece of paper and cut it out.
- On the footprint, they draw or write one action they will take to be a role model (e.g., "I will help someone who's feeling left out" or "I will follow the rules even when others don't").
- Create a path of footprints along the wall or hallway to show how role models lead the way.

End-of-Week Reflection:

- What did I do this week to be a role model?

- Who might have been influenced by my actions?

- How did it feel to lead by example?

PART FOUR

EMPOWERING STUDENT LEADERSHIP

Being a leader isn't just about being in charge—it's about showing others what's possible by the way you carry yourself.

In this section, students will discover what leadership really means in everyday life—whether it's in the classroom, with friends, or at home. They'll learn how to manage their own choices, set healthy boundaries, lift others up, and make decisions that line up with their values.

Together, we'll explore what it looks like to lead with empathy, courage, and integrity. This isn't about having all the answers—it's about being someone others can trust, someone who takes initiative, and someone who helps build a community where everyone feels seen, safe, and supported.

WEEK 31:

SERVICE TO OTHERS

"Sometimes it's the smallest sparkle that makes the biggest difference."
—Thema the Unicorn

Learn:

Service means helping others simply because you care. It's doing something kind without expecting anything back. It could be helping someone carry their things, sharing your toys, or helping clean up after lunch. Every time we serve others, we make the world a little brighter.

Consider:

Imagine your friend drops their crayons on the floor. You stop what you're doing and help them pick them up. You didn't do it for a reward—you just cared. That small act of service made your friend feel seen and supported.

Let's Make It Real:

Talk to the person next to you about a time when someone helped you. What did they do, and how did it make you feel?

Discuss:

- Why is it important to help others even if we don't get anything in return?
- How do acts of service make our classroom a better place?
- What are some kind things you can do to help others this week?

Do:

This week, look for ways to serve others. That might mean helping a classmate, cleaning up, or giving someone a compliment. Notice how your kindness helps others feel good.

Activity:

Sparkle Jar of Kindness

- Set up a jar in the classroom and cut out lots of small stars or sparkles.
- When a student sees someone doing an act of service, they can write it on a sparkle and put it in the jar.
- At the end of the week, read some aloud to celebrate how everyone is making a difference!

End-of-Week Reflection:

- How did I serve others this week?

- Did I help someone feel seen or cared for?

- What did I learn about how even small acts of service can make a big difference?

WEEK 32:

MENTORING PEERS

"You're braver than you believe, and stronger than you seem,
and smarter than you think."
—Christopher Robin

Learn:

Being a mentor means helping a friend when they're stuck, sharing what you know, and cheering them on. You don't need to be the oldest or the best at something to be a mentor. You just need to care, listen, and be kind. When you help others learn, you grow too!

Consider:

Imagine your friend is learning to play the recorder in music class, but they're getting frustrated. Instead of grabbing the recorder and playing it for them, you sit beside them and show them how to hold it and where to place their fingers. You cheer them on until they play the notes on their own. That's what being a mentor looks like—helping someone believe they can do it.

Let's Make It Real:

Talk to the person next to you about a time when someone helped you learn something new. What did they do to help you?

Discuss:

- Why is it helpful to have someone mentor us?
- How can we be a mentor to someone who's struggling?
- What's something you could teach or show to someone else?

Do:

This week, look for a time when you can be a mentor. Maybe someone needs help with reading, packing up, or learning the rules of a game. Use your kindness and patience to guide them.

Activity:

Mentor Moments Journal

- Create a simple journal page for students with two sections:
    1. *Today I helped someone by...*
    2. *Today someone helped me by...*
- Throughout the week, students write or draw in their journal when they mentor someone or receive help.

- At the end of the week, reflect as a class and celebrate how mentoring helped everyone learn and grow.

End-of-Week Reflection:

- Did I help someone learn or feel more confident this week?
- How did mentoring feel?
- What did I learn from teaching or supporting someone else?

WEEK 33:

PRIORITY MANAGEMENT FOR SUCCESS

"First, we eat. Then, we go see Grandma."
—Anna, *Frozen II*

Learn:

Priority management means choosing what's most important and doing that first. Sometimes we have lots of things to do—schoolwork, playing, helping at home—and we can feel overwhelmed. When we make a plan and do the important things first, we feel proud and calm.

Consider:

Imagine you have homework to finish, but you start playing with your toys instead. By the time you remember your homework, it's bedtime! You feel rushed and stressed. But if you had done your homework first, you would've had time to play and feel proud that your work was done. That's what managing priorities looks like.

Let's Make It Real:

Talk to the person next to you about a time when you did the important thing first. How did it help you? Or talk about a time when you didn't, and how that felt.

Discuss:

- Why is it helpful to do the important things first?
- What happens when we ignore our priorities?
- What's one thing you need to do this week before having free time?

Do:

This week, make a short list of things you need to do each day. Put a star next to the most important one and start with that.

Activity:

Classroom Priority Sorting Game

- Create cards with classroom tasks (e.g., finishing morning work, unpacking your bag, sharpening pencils, helping a friend, lining up for lunch, colouring a picture, choosing a book, chatting with a classmate).
- In small groups or as a class, have students sort the cards into two categories: "Important to do first" and "Can wait until later."

- Discuss why some tasks need to be done right away and how it helps the day go smoothly.

- Extension: Invite students to create their own cards that show their daily classroom responsibilities and routines.

End-of-Week Reflection:

- Did I complete my important tasks this week?

- How did it feel to do those things first?

- What did I learn about planning my time?

WEEK 34:

PROBLEM-SOLVING SKILLS

"If we want to save this world, creativity is the key to survival."
—STEVE, MINECRAFT: THE MOVIE

Learn:

Problem-solving means finding a way to fix something that's not working. It's like being a detective—looking at the clues, staying calm, and trying different ideas until something works. You don't have to fix things alone. Working together and listening to others can help you find even better answers.

Consider:

Imagine you and your friends are playing a game at lunch and accidentally break a window. Everyone feels scared and unsure what to do. One person says, "Let's go tell the teacher together and explain what happened." You all agree, and even though it's hard, you take responsibility and help clean up. That's problem-solving—being honest, working together, and making a plan to fix the problem.

Let's Make It Real:

Talk to the person next to you about a time when you had to solve a problem. What did you try? What worked?

Discuss:

- Why is it important to stay calm when there's a problem?
- Can you think of a time when trying something new helped you solve a challenge?
- How can working with others help you solve problems better?

Do:

This week, if something gets tricky, take a deep breath and think like a problem-solver. Try one step at a time, ask for ideas, and don't give up.

Activity:

Egg Parachute Challenge

- Give students materials like string, plastic bags, tape, and paper to design a parachute that will protect an egg from breaking when dropped.
- Students work in teams to plan, build, and test their parachutes.
- After each drop, teams reflect on what worked and what they could improve.

- This hands-on challenge helps students practise teamwork, creative thinking, and trying different solutions when something doesn't go right.

End-of-Week Reflection:

- What problem did I solve this week?
- What steps helped me figure it out?
- How did solving a problem make me feel?

WEEK 35:

EMPOWERING CHOICES

"In our family, everyone gets a turn to be the leader, even Bingo!"
—Bluey

Learn:

Empowering choices are decisions that help others feel free and re-spected. A powerful person doesn't try to control others—they support people in making their own choices. When we allow others to decide for themselves and don't boss them around, we create safe and kind spaces. Being powerful means taking care of your own actions and giving others the freedom to do the same.

Consider:

Imagine you're working in a group and one person wants to do things their own way. Instead of trying to take over and tell everyone what to do, you ask, "What do you think we should try first?" That's a powerful choice—giving others a voice and working together. A powerless choice would be ignoring their ideas and trying to control everything yourself.

Let's Make It Real:

Talk to the person next to you about a time when you let someone else make a choice instead of telling them what to do. How do you think they felt? How did it feel for you to be a powerful leader who gave others freedom?

Discuss:

- Why is it important to let others make their own choices?
- Can you think of a time when someone let you choose and how did you feel?
- How can we support our friends without trying to control them?

Do:

This week, focus on being a leader who makes space for others to make their own choices. Instead of controlling, listen and consider their perspective. Ask things like, "What do you think?" or "How can I support you?" Notice how this helps everyone feel safe and respected.

Activity:

Make a Sandwich––Leadership Style!

- In pairs, each student makes a real sandwich using bread, butter, and a spread that the teacher provides (e.g., jam, honey, or Vegemite). If using food isn't possible, keep it as a pretend activity.

- The first student makes their sandwich step by step, explaining what they are doing. The partner watches and doesn't interrupt, even if it's different from how they'd do it.

- Then they swap roles. The second student makes their sandwich their own way while the first partner watches and learns.

- After both have finished, talk about how it felt to let someone do it their way and not step in to control them. Consider how your sandwiches were made differently—did it really matter? Did each person still end up with something they liked?

- Discuss how this is like letting others make their own choices and being a supportive leader.

End-of-Week Reflection:

- What powerful choices did I make this week?

- How did I give others freedom to choose?

- How did it feel to be a leader who supported others instead of trying to control them?

- What have I learned about being a powerful person?

WEEK 36:

HEALTHY BOUNDARIES
IN LEADERSHIP

"No, that's too rough!"
—BINGO, *BLUEY*

Learn:

Healthy boundaries in leadership mean knowing what you're okay with and what you're not, and respecting what others are okay with too. Great leaders know when to say yes, and when to say no. They don't try to do everything or control everyone. Instead, they help others share the job and make space for everyone to feel safe and heard.

Consider:

Imagine you're the leader of a group game and you're trying to keep everything fair. One person keeps changing the rules, and it's making things confusing. You stop and say, "Let's stick to the rules we all agreed on, so everyone can enjoy playing." That's setting a healthy boundary— you didn't get angry or bossy, but you helped the group stay on track.

Let's Make It Real:

Talk to the person next to you about a time when you said what you were okay with in a kind way. How did that help the situation? Have you ever been glad that someone set a boundary with you?

Discuss:

- Why is it helpful to set boundaries as a leader?
- How can we set boundaries without being mean or bossy?
- What can we say if someone crosses a boundary?

Do:

This week, focus on setting healthy boundaries when you need to. Use kind words to share how you feel and what you need. Notice how that helps you stay calm and keep your friendships strong.

Activity:

Bubble Boundaries Game

- Give each student a hula hoop or imaginary bubble space around them.
- As a class, walk around and practise moving through the room without bumping into each other's bubbles.

- Then stop and pair up. One person practises saying, "No thank you, I need space," and the other practises respecting that boundary.
- Talk about how it felt to ask for space and to give it.

End-of-Week Reflection:

- Did I set any healthy boundaries this week?
- How did it feel to say what I was okay with?
- What did I learn about being a respectful and kind leader?

WEEK 37:

CELEBRATING SUCCESSES TOGETHER

"There is no 'I' in team!"
— Mr. Incredible, *The Incredibles*

Learn:

Being a leader means noticing when something has gone well and making sure everyone feels proud—not just yourself. Celebrating successes together helps your team feel happy, connected, and ready for more challenges. Good leaders share the joy and say, "Well done!" to others.

Consider:

Imagine your class works hard on a big art project. Everyone puts in effort and it turns out amazing! Instead of just saying, "I did great," a good leader says, "We all did great!" and finds a fun way to celebrate together. That kind of leader makes everyone feel important.

Let's Make It Real:

Talk to the person next to you about a time when you celebrated with your class or family. What did you do to celebrate? How did it feel to enjoy the moment together?

Discuss:

- Why is it important to celebrate other people's successes?
- How do you feel when someone notices your hard work?
- What can you do to be a leader who celebrates others?

Do:

This week, be a leader who looks out for success in others. When someone does something well—big or small—say something kind or cheer them on. Notice how it makes them feel, and how it makes your team stronger.

Activity:

Team Shout-Out Chain

- Sit in a circle as a class.
- One person gives a shout-out to someone else for something they did well that week (e.g., helping, working hard, being kind).
- That person then gives a shout-out to someone else, and so on until everyone has been recognised.
- Finish with a class cheer or special celebration (like a class dance) to celebrate the team!

End-of-Week Reflection:

- Who did I celebrate this week?

- How do you feel when you recognise others?

- What did I learn about being a leader who lifts others up?

WEEK 38:

ENCOURAGING GROWTH
IN OTHERS

"Venture outside your comfort zone. The rewards are worth it."
—Rapunzel, *Tangled*

Learn:

Leaders don't just work on their own growth—they help others grow too! Encouraging growth in others means cheering people on when they're learning something new, helping them when they're stuck, and reminding them they can do hard things. A great leader sees potential in others and helps them shine.

Consider:

Imagine a friend is learning to play the recorder in music class but feels nervous. You say, "You're doing better each day! Want to practise together?" That support can help them feel more confident and ready to keep trying. Leaders know that a little encouragement can make a big difference.

Let's Make It Real:

Talk to the person next to you about a time when someone encouraged you to try something new. How did that help you grow? Or, share a time you helped someone else feel brave.

Discuss:

- Why is it important to help others grow?
- What does it feel like when someone cheers you on?
- What can you say to someone who feels nervous about trying something new?

Do:

This week, be a leader who encourages others. If you see someone trying something hard, say something kind or offer to help. Notice how your words and actions can help someone feel brave and keep going.

Activity:

Paper Garden of Growth

- Each student gets a paper flower.
- On the petals, they write or draw something someone said or did this week that encouraged them.
- Decorate and display the flowers on a classroom wall to make a garden.

- Take time as a class to visit the garden and celebrate how leaders helped each other grow.

End-of-Week Reflection:
- Who did I encourage this week?
- How did it feel to support someone else's growth?
- What did I learn about being a leader who helps others grow?

WEEK 39:

HANDLING DISAPPOINTMENT

*"The flower that blooms in adversity is the
most rare and beautiful of all."*
—The Emperor, *Mulan*

Learn:

Even great leaders feel disappointed sometimes. Maybe something
doesn't go the way you hoped, or you didn't get picked for a team or
prize. Handling disappointment means not giving up. It means learning
from what happened, trying again, and becoming stronger because of it.

Consider:

Imagine you really wanted to win a classroom game, but your team
didn't win. At first, you feel upset. But instead of staying sad, you cheer
on the winning team and think about how you could do better next time.
That's what a strong leader does—feel the feelings, and then keep going.

Let's Make It Real:

Talk to the person next to you about a time you felt disappointed. What did you do next? How did you move forward?

Discuss:

- Why do we sometimes feel disappointed?
- What can we learn when things don't go our way?
- How can leaders show others how to handle disappointment kindly and bravely?

Do:

This week, if something doesn't go how you hoped, stop and take a breath. Remind yourself that this is a chance to grow, and think about one thing you can do differently next time.

Activity:

Disappointment-to-Victory Chart

- Draw two columns on a piece of paper. Label the first column "Disappointment" and the second one "Victory."
- Think about a time when you felt disappointed (for example, not winning a game or not getting a reward).
- In the "Disappointment" column, write or draw what happened.
- In the "Victory" column, write or draw how you bounced back or what you learned from the situation. (For example, you kept trying, asked for help, or learned a new skill).

- Share your charts with a partner or small group to show how you turned disappointment into a chance to grow.

End-of-Week Reflection:

- What was one disappointment I faced this week?
- What did I do to bounce back?
- What did I learn about myself when things didn't go my way?

WEEK 40:

CELEBRATING GROWTH

"Our fate lives within us. You only have to be brave enough to see it."
—Princess Merida, Brave

Learn:

Celebrating growth means recognising how much you've changed and improved, even if you're not at your final goal yet. Growth isn't just about reaching the finish line—it's about every small step you take to get there. By celebrating how far you've come, you feel more confident and excited to keep going!

Consider:

Think about what we've learned together this year about building a strong classroom culture. We've worked on building healthy relationships, being responsible, and restoring relationships when messes get made. Every time we practice these skills, we're growing individually and as a class. Just like how a garden grows little by little, we've been working on growing our class culture, and each step counts. When we celebrate our progress, we build more momentum to keep going!

Let's Make It Real:

Talk to the person next to you about something you've improved on this year. What new skills have you learned? How did these help you?

Discuss:

- Why is it important to celebrate our growth as a class?
- Can you think of a time this year when celebrating growth motivated you to keep going toward a bigger goal?
- How can you help your friends celebrate their growth?

Do:

This week, think about something you've gotten better at—whether it's a skill in school, a new thing you've learned, or something you've worked hard to improve. Take a moment to celebrate it. Share what you've achieved with a friend or family member and be proud of how far you've come!

Activity:

Rate and Grow Challenge

- Take a moment to rate yourself on one of the following:
    - How I am doing in my friendships (1-10)

- How I am doing taking responsibility for myself (1-10)
- How I am doing cleaning up my messes and restoring friendships (1-10)
- After rating yourself, think of one thing you can do to improve by 1 point. Write it down or tell someone!
  - Example: "I'm going to ask a friend if they need help" or "I will do my work in class and talk with my friends at lunch."
- Share your goal with a friend, and let them know how they can help you celebrate your progress!

End-of-Week Reflection:

- How did I celebrate my growth this week? Did I celebrate someone else's growth?
- What did I contribute to our class culture growth this year?
- How can I take what I have learned into next year's classroom?

BONUS TOPICS

Think of this Bonus Section as some extra goodness for those weeks when the term runs a little longer than usual!

These extra sessions are designed to build on everything students have already learned—giving them more chances to reflect, grow, and keep building their leadership muscles. Whether it's diving deeper into responsibility, strengthening relationships, or growing in personal confidence, these sessions offer fresh challenges and meaningful conversations to keep the momentum going.

It's all about continuing the journey and giving students more space to grow into the powerful, respectful, and connected people they're becoming.

BONUS

CHOICES AND CONSEQUENCES

"The call isn't out there at all; it's inside me."
— MOANA, *MOANA*

Learn:

Every choice we make has a consequence, whether we notice it right away or not. Some choices give us rewards quickly, like earning a sticker after finishing a task, while others take time, like building trust with our friends by being kind. When we understand that our choices shape our lives, we can make better decisions and enjoy the results!

Consider:

Imagine one student talks during a lesson and misses out on important information. They feel confused later because they didn't pay attention. Another student chooses to focus on the lesson and finishes their work, earning praise from the teacher. Both students made choices, but their results were very different because of those choices.

Let's Make It Real:

Talk to the person next to you about a time when a choice you made had a consequence—either good or bad. How did that outcome affect you or others?

Discuss:

- Can you think of a recent choice you made and what the outcome was?
- Why is it important to think about consequences before making a decision?
- How can good choices lead to better results in school or friendships?

Do:

This week, before making a decision, pause and think about what could happen because of that choice. Afterward, reflect on how your decision affected you or others. Ask yourself: Was this a good choice? What did I learn?

Activity:

Choice and Consequence Wheel

- Draw a big circle and divide it into sections like a pizza. Label each section with a different choice, like "help a friend," "focus on schoolwork," "talk during class," "wait your turn," etc.

- In each section, draw or write the consequences of that choice (good or bad). For example: "Help a friend – They'll be happy and might help me next time!" or "Talk during class – Miss important information."

- Spin the wheel and pick a choice to talk about. Discuss what the consequence could be and how it could make you feel.

End-of-Week Reflection:

- What choices did you make this week, and how did they affect you?

- Were there any surprises, either good or bad?

- What did you learn about thinking before making a choice?

BONUS

SETTING PERSONAL GOALS

"You don't have to be perfect to be amazing!"
— Wreck-It Ralph

Learn:

Setting personal goals means deciding what you want to achieve and making a plan to reach it. Goals help us stay focused, motivated, and on track. Whether you want to improve at something, learn something new, or be a better friend, setting goals helps you grow and be proud of your progress.

Consider:

Imagine a student wants to get better at reading, so they set a goal to read 20 minutes every day. At first, it feels like a lot, but as they keep practicing, they read faster and feel more confident. Setting that goal helped them become better at something they cared about.

Let's Make It Real:

Talk to the person next to you about a goal you've set in the past or one you'd like to set for the future. How do you plan to achieve it?

Discuss:

- Why is setting goals important, and how does it help us focus?
- Can you think of a time when setting a goal helped you accomplish something?
- What goal can you set for yourself that will help you grow?

Do:

This week, set a personal goal for yourself! Whether it's reading for 10 minutes a day, winning a game of chess against your dad, or learning an instrument, choose something you'd like to improve. Write it down, share it with a friend, and check in on your progress each day.

Activity:

Jumping for Goals

1. **Step 1:** Find a clear space where you can jump.
2. **Step 2:** Jump as far as you can, then mark where your feet land with a piece of tape or chalk on the floor.
3. **Step 3:** Now, make it your goal to jump farther than your mark. Take a few moments to focus and think about how you can jump farther, and then give it your all.
4. **Step 4:** Most people will be able to jump farther because they have a goal to aim for. This is why goal setting can be so helpful.

End-of-Week Reflection:

- Did you set a goal this week? How did you work toward it?
- What challenges did you face, and how did your goal help you keep going?
- What did you learn about the power of setting goals?

BONUS

INCLUSION AND DIVERSITY

"The things that make me different are the things that make me."
—DUMBO, *DUMBO*

Learn:

Inclusion means making sure everyone feels welcome, no matter who they are. Diversity means appreciating what makes us different, whether it's where we come from, what we like, or how we look. When we celebrate diversity and include everyone, we create a kind, respectful environment where we can all grow and learn from each other.

Consider:

Imagine you're playing a game with your friends, and you notice that one classmate is sitting alone. Instead of leaving them out, you invite them to join the game. By including everyone, you make sure your classmate feels welcome and valued. When everyone is included, your group becomes stronger and more fun.

Let's Make It Real:

Talk to the person next to you about a time when you were included in a group, or when you included someone else. How did it make everyone feel?

Discuss:

- Why is it important to include people who are different from us?
- Can you think of a time when diversity helped you see things in a new way?
- How can you make an effort to include others at school?

Do:

This week, look for chances to include someone who might feel left out. Notice how your group becomes stronger and more positive when everyone is included.

Activity:

The Continuum of Likes and Dislikes

Objective: This interactive activity will help students understand and appreciate diversity by showing how we all have different preferences, yet all of our opinions are valuable.

1. **Set the Scene:** Mark a line across the room or basketball court with "I Love" on one end and "I Don't Like" on the other.

2. **Instructions:** Explain that you will ask a series of questions, and for each question, students will stand somewhere on the line based on how much they like or dislike something:

   - If they really love something, they stand closer to the "I Love" side.
   - If they really don't like something, they stand closer to the "I Don't Like" side.
   - If they're unsure, they can stand somewhere in the middle.

3. **Ask Questions:** Example questions to ask the students:

   - "How do you feel about spaghetti?"
   - "Do you like cleaning your room?"
   - "How do you feel about baking with mum?"
   - "Do you like playing sports?"
   - "Do you like chocolate?"

4. **Encourage Sharing:** After each question, ask a few students to share why they stood where they did. This shows that everyone's likes and dislikes are different, and that's what makes us unique.

5. **Discuss:** After the activity, ask the students:

   - "How did it feel to stand on the line with others who have the same likes and dislikes as you?"
   - "What was it like to stand near someone who had different preferences from you?"
   - "How can we respect each other's differences in the classroom?"

End-of-Week Reflection:

- How did you include others this week?

- Were there moments when you appreciated your group's diversity?

- What did you learn about inclusion and valuing differences?

BONUS

HANDLING PEER PRESSURE

"There is no secret ingredient. It's just you."
—Po, *Kung Fu Panda*

Learn:

Peer pressure happens when people try to get you to do something because they are doing it, or because they want you to fit in with the group. It can make you feel like you have to do something you're not comfortable with, even if it's not the right choice for you. Handling peer pressure means knowing what is best for you and making your own decisions, even when others are trying to influence you.

Consider:

Imagine you are playing a game with your friends, and they want you to play in a way that doesn't feel right to you, like breaking a rule.

Even though you might want to fit in, you choose to keep playing by the rules and show your friends that you can still have fun without breaking them.

Let's Make It Real:

Talk to the person next to you about a time when you felt pressure to do something just because everyone else was doing it. How did you feel, and what did you do? Did you stand up for what you thought was right?

Discuss:

- Why is it important to stay true to yourself, even when others want you to do something different?
- Can you think of a time when peer pressure helped you make a good choice? Or a time it led to something you regretted?
- What are some ways to handle peer pressure if it happens at school or with your friends?

Do:

This week, when you feel peer pressure, remember that it's okay to make your own decisions. Whether it's in a game or when you're with friends, trust yourself and make choices that feel right to you.

Activity:

Peer Pressure Bingo

Objective: To help students identify situations where they might face peer pressure and think about how to handle them.

1. **Set the Scene:** Explain to the class that peer pressure can happen in many different situations. Sometimes, it's easy to say "yes" when everyone else says "yes," but it's important to think for yourself and make the best decision. You can stand by your values and say "no" when something doesn't feel right.

2. **Instructions:**

- Give each student a **Peer Pressure Bingo Card** (you can create a simple grid with squares, each containing a different situation where peer pressure might occur).

- Examples of situations to include on the Bingo Card:

  - "Someone offers you candy, but you're not hungry."

  - "A friend wants you to skip class."

  - "You're told to ignore a new student."

  - "Everyone is making fun of someone, and they want you to join in."

  - "A group wants you to break something just for fun."

  - "Someone tells you to lie to a teacher."

3. **How to Play:**

  - Students go around the room and discuss the scenarios with a partner or in small groups, reflecting on whether they've ever been in that situation or if they can think of a better way to handle it.

  - As they discuss, they mark off the squares on their Bingo card where they can relate or where they've seen peer pressure happen.

  - The goal is for students to complete a row, column, or diagonal by identifying situations they've experienced or could relate to.

4. **Discuss:**

- After the activity, gather the class together and ask them to reflect on their answers.

- How would you handle each situation on your Bingo card?

- Why is it important to make your own choices and stand up for what's right?

- How can we help our friends resist peer pressure?

End-of-Week Reflection:

- How did I handle peer pressure this week?

- Did I make a decision that felt true to me, even if others disagreed?

- What did I learn about the power of making my own choices?

EQUIPPING A CULTURE OF LOVE

At Godwin Consulting, we believe in empowering educators and leaders to create environments where joy, responsibility and connection thrive. That's why we've designed a variety of resources to support you on your journey—whether you're working with students, staff, or leaders.

If you're looking to bring lasting change to your school, our LoSoP Foundations Course (online, self-paced) and LoSoP School Representative Programs (facilitated) offer tailored, in-depth training to guide you every step of the way. Whether you're looking to lead with joy and responsibility or turn your classroom into a space of growth and respect, we've got the tools, knowledge, and support to make it happen.

Our resources are all about making your day easier and more impactful. From practical classroom tools like our LoSoP Desk Flip and Diagram or Language Flashcards to our empowering Umbrella of Grace, each item is designed to bring connection and grace to your everyday teaching. We also have printable posters to help you keep the LoSoP philosophy front and centre in your work, plus online courses that dig deeper into the LoSoP principles and give you practical, actionable strategies.

Explore our website and find the resources that can make a difference in your school culture today. We're here to support you on your mission to nurture stronger, more connected communities.

Check out our online store at **www.godwinconsulting.com.au**

ABOUT THE AUTHOR

Bernii Godwin holds a Master's qualification in Social Work and a Graduate Certificate in Neuropsychotherapy, building on her undergraduate degree in Human Services and Criminology and Criminal Justice, with a focus on youth and family justice. She is also a certified Loving on Purpose Trainer and John Maxwell Leadership Team Member.

Over the past two decades, Bernii has worked in various roles across a wide range of schools, specializing in student well-being and behaviour. Principals frequently seek her expertise to consult on complex behaviour and well-being issues, provide one-on-one coaching or supervision to educators and well-being teams, and deliver school-wide professional development. Her greatest passion is helping schools adopt practical tools that replace fear and punishment with purposeful behaviour education, safe connections, and empowered teachers—ultimately increasing student engagement in their academic journey.

To connect with Bernii, please visit:
www.godwinconsulting.com.au

www.ingramcontent.com/pod-product-compliance
Lightning Source LLC
Chambersburg PA
CBHW070149310326
41914CB00089B/659